THE PRISONER OF CHILLON

Written by
Lord Byron

Edited by
Ernest Hartley Coleridge

2015

Table of Contents

INTRODUCTION TO THE PRISONER OF CHILLON.

The Prisoner of Chillon, says Moore (Life, p. 320), was written at Ouchy, near Lausanne, where Byron and Shelley "were detained two days in a small inn by the weather." Byron's letter to Murray, dated June 27 (but? 28), 1816, does not precisely tally with Shelley's journal contained in a letter to Peacock, July 12, 1816 (Prose Works of P. B. Shelley, 1880, ii. 171, sq.); but, if Shelley's first date, June 23, is correct, it follows that the two poets visited the Castle of Chillon on Wednesday, June 26, reached Ouchy on Thursday, June 27, and began their homeward voyage on Saturday, June 29 (Shelley misdates it June 30). On this reckoning the Prisoner of Chillon was begun and finished between Thursday, June 27, and Saturday, June 29, 1816. Whenever or wherever begun, it was completed by July 10 (see Memoir of John Murray, 1891, i. 364), and was ready for transmission to England by July 25. The MS., in Claire's handwriting, was placed in Murray's hands on October 11, and the poem, with seven others, was published December 5, 1816.

In a final note to the Prisoner of Chillon (First Edition, 1816, p. 59), Byron confesses that when "the foregoing poem was composed he knew too little of the history of Bonnivard to do justice to his courage and virtues," and appends as a note to the "Sonnet on Chillon," "some account of his life ... furnished by the kindness of a citizen of that Republic," i.e. Geneva. The note, which is now entitled "Advertisement," is taken bodily from the pages of a work published in 1786 by the Swiss naturalist, Jean Senebier, who died in 1809. It was not Byron's way to invent imaginary authorities, but rather to give his references with some pride and particularity, and it is possible that this unacknowledged and hitherto unverified "account" was supplied by some literary acquaintance, who failed to explain that his information was common property. Be that as it may, Senebier's prose is in some respects as unhistorical as Byron's verse, and stands in need of some corrections and additions.

François Bonivard (there is no contemporary authority for "Bonnivard") was born in 1493. In early youth (1510) he became by inheritance Prior of St. Victor, a monastery outside the walls of Geneva, and on reaching manhood (1514) he accepted the office and the benefice, "la dignité ecclésiastique de Prieur et de la Seigneurie temporelle de St. Victor." A lover of independence, a child of the later Renaissance, in a word, a Genevese, he threw in his lot with a band of ardent reformers and patriots, who were conspiring to shake off the yoke of Duke Charles III. of Savoy, and convert the city into a republic. Here is his own testimony: "Dès que j'eus commencé de lire l'histoire des nations, je me sentis entrainé par un goût prononcé pour les Républiques dont j'épousai toujours les intérêts." Hence, in a great measure, the unrelenting enmity of the duke, who not only ousted him from his priory, but caused him to be shut up for two years at Grolée, Gex, and Belley, and again, after he had been liberated on a second occasion, ordered him, a safe conduct notwithstanding, to be seized and confined in the Castle of Chillon. Here he remained from 1530 to February 1, 1536, when he was released by the Bernese.

For the first two years he was lodged in a room near the governor's quarters, and was fairly comfortable; but a day came when the duke paid a visit to Chillon; and "then," he writes, "the captain thrust me into a cell lower than the lake, where I lived four years. I know not whether he did it by the duke's orders or of his own accord; but sure it is that I had so much leisure for walking, that I wore in the rock which was the pavement a track or little path, as it had been made with a hammer" (Chroniques des Ligues de Stumpf, addition de Bonivard).

After he had been liberated, "par la grace de Dieu donnee a Messrs de Berne," he returned to Geneva, and was made a member of the Council of the State, and awarded a house and a pension of two hundred crowns a year. A long life was before him, which he proceeded to spend in characteristic fashion, finely and honourably as scholar, author, and reformer, but with little self-regard or self-respect as a private citizen. He was married no less than four times, and not one of these alliances was altogether satisfactory or creditable. Determined "to warm both hands before the fire of life," he was prone to ignore the prejudices and even the decencies of his fellow-citizens, now incurring their displeasure, and now again, as one who had greatly testified for truth and freedom, being taken back into favour and forgiven. There was a deal of human nature in Bonivard, with the result that, at times, conduct fell short of pretension and principle. Estimates of his character differ widely. From the standpoint of Catholic orthodoxy, "C'était un fort mauvais sujet et un plus mauvais prêtre;" and even his captivity, infamous as it was, "ne peut rendre Bonivard intéressant" (Notices Généalogiques sur les Famillies Genevoises, par J. A. Galiffe, 1836, iii. 67, sq.); whilst an advocate and champion, the author of the Preface to Les Chroniques de Genève par François de Bonnivard, 1831, tom. i. pt. i. p. xli., avows that "aucun homme n'a fait preuve d'un plus beau caractère, d'un plus parfait désintéressement que l'illustre Prieur de St. Victor." Like other great men, he may have been guilty of "quelques égaremens du coeur, quelques concessions passagères aux dévices des sens," but "Peu importe à la postérité les irrégularités de leur vie privée" (p. xlviii.).

But whatever may be the final verdict with regard to the morals, there can be no question as to the intellectual powers of the "Prisoner of Chillon." The publication of various MS. tracts, e.g. Advis et Devis de l'ancienne et nouvelle Police de Genève, 1865; Advis et Devis des Lengnes, etc., 1865, which were edited by the late J. J. Chaponnière, and, after his death, by M. Gustave Revilliod, has placed his reputation as historian, satirist, philosopher, beyond doubt or cavil. One quotation must suffice. He is contrasting the Protestants with the Catholics (Advis et Devis de la Source de Lidolatrie, Geneva, 1856, p. 159): "Et nous disons que les prebstres rongent les mortz et est vray; mais nous faisons bien pys, car nous rongeons les vifz. Quel profit revient aux paveures du dommage des prebstres? Nous nous ventons touttes les deux parties de prescher Christ cruciffie et disons vray, car nous le laissons cruciffie et nud en l'arbre de la croix, et jouons a beaux dez au pied dicelle croix, pour scavoir qui haura sa robe."

For Bonivard's account of his second imprisonment, see Les Chroniques de Genève, tom. ii. part ii. pp. 571-577; see, too, Notice sur François Bonivard, ...par Le Docteur J. J. Chaponnière, Mémoires et Documents Publiés, par La Société d'Histoire, etc., de Genève, 1845, iv. 137-245; Chillon Etude Historique, par L. Vulliemin, Lausanne, 1851; Revue des Deux Mondes, Seconde Période, vol. 82, Août, 1869, pp. 682-709; "True Story of the Prisoner of Chillon," Nineteenth Century, May, 1900, No. 279, pp. 821-829, by A. van Amstel (Johannes Christiaan Neuman).

The Prisoner of Chillon was reviewed (together with the Third Canto of Childe Harold) by Sir Walter Scott (Quarterly Review, No. xxxi., October, 1816), and by Jeffrey (Edinburgh Review, No. liv., December, 1816).

With the exception of the Eclectic (March, 1817, N.S., vol. vii. pp. 298-304), the lesser reviews were unfavourable. For instance, the Critical Review (December, 1816, Series V. vol. iv. pp. 567-581) detected the direct but unacknowledged influence of Wordsworth on thought and style; and thePortfolio (No. vi. pp. 121-128), in an elaborate skit, entitled "Literary Frauds," assumed, and affected to prove, that the entire poem was a forgery, and belonged to the same category as The Right Honourable Lord Byron's Pilgrimage to the Holy Land, etc.

For extracts from these and other reviews, see Kölbing, Prisoner of Chillon, and Other Poems, Weimar, 1896, excursus i. pp. 3-55.

SONNET ON CHILLON

ETERNAL Spirit of the chainless Mind!
Brightest in dungeons, Liberty! thou art:
For there thy habitation is the heart—
The heart which love of thee alone can bind;
And when thy sons to fetters are consigned—
To fetters, and the damp vault's dayless gloom,
Their country conquers with their martyrdom,
And Freedom's fame finds wings on every wind.
Chillon! thy prison is a holy place,
And thy sad floor an altar—for 'twas trod,
Until his very steps have left a trace
Worn, as if thy cold pavement were a sod,
By Bonnivard!—May none those marks efface!
For they appeal from tyranny to God.

ADVERTISEMENT

WHEN this poem was composed, I was not sufficiently aware of the history of Bonnivard, or I should have endeavoured to dignify the subject by an attempt to celebrate his courage and his virtues. With some account of his life I have been furnished, by the kindness of a citizen of that republic, which is still proud of the memory of a man worthy of the best age of ancient freedom: —

"François De Bonnivard, fils de Louis De Bonnivard, originaire de Seyssel et Seigneur de Lunes, naquit en 1496. Il fit ses études à Turin: en 1510 Jean Aimé de Bonnivard, son oncle, lui résigna le Prieuré de St. Victor, qui aboutissoit aux murs de Genève, et qui formait un bénéfice considérable....

"Ce grand homme — (Bonnivard mérite ce litre par la force de son âme, la droiture de son coeur, la noblesse de ses intentions, la sagesse de ses conseils, le courage de ses démarches, l'étendue de ses connaissances, et la vivacité de son esprit), — ce grand homme, qui excitera l'admiration de tous ceux qu'une vertu héroïque peut encore émouvoir, inspirera encore la plus vive reconnaissance dans les coeurs des Genevois qui aiment Genève. Bonnivard en fut toujours un des plus fermes appuis: pour assurer la liberté de notre République, il ne craignit pas de perdre souvent la sienne; il oublia son repos; il méprisa ses richesses; il ne négligea rien pour affermir le bonheur d'une patrie qu'il honora de son choix: dès ce moment il la chérit comme le plus zélé de ses citoyens; il la servit avec l'intrépidité d'un héros, et il écrivit son Histoire avec la naïveté d'un philosophe et la chaleur d'un patriote.

"Il dit dans le commencement de son Histoire de Genève, que, dès qu'il eut commencé de lire l'histoire des nations, il se sentit entraîné par son goût pour les Républiques, dont il épousa toujours les intérêts: c'est ce goût pour la liberté qui lui fit sans doute adopter Genève pour sa patrie....

"Bonnivard, encore jeune, s'annonça hautement comme le défenseur de Genève contre le Duc de Savoye et l'Evêque....

"En 1519, Bonnivard devient le martyr de sa patrie: Le Duc de Savoye étant entré dans Genève avec cinq cent hommes, Bonnivard craint le ressentiment du Duc; il voulut se retirer à Fribourg pour en éviter les suites; mais il fut trahi par deux hommes qui l'accompagnaient, et conduit par ordre du Prince à Grolée, où il resta prisonnier pendant deux ans. Bonnivard était malheureux dans ses voyages: comme ses malheurs n'avaient point ralenti son zèle pour Genève, il était toujours un ennemi redoutable pour ceux qui la menaçaient, et par conséquent il devait être exposé à leurs coups. Il fut rencontré en 1530 sur le Jura par des voleurs, qui le dépouillèrent, et qui le mirent encore entre les mains du Duc de Savoye: ce Prince le fit enfermer dans le Château de Chillon, où il resta sans être interrogé jusques en 1536; il fut alors delivré par les Bernois, qui s'emparèrent du Pays-de-Vaud.

"Bonnivard, en sortant de sa captivité, eut le plaisir de trouver Genève libre et réformée: la République s'empressa de lui témoigner sa reconnaissance, et de le dédommager des maux qu'il avoit soufferts; elle le reçut Bourgeois de la ville au mois de Juin, 1536; elle lui donna la maison habitée autrefois par le Vicaire-Général, et elle lui assigna une pension de deux cent écus d'or tant qu'il séjournerait à Genève. Il fut admis dans le Conseil des Deux-Cent en 1537.

"Bonnivard n'a pas fini d'être utile: après avoir travaillé à rendre Genève libre, il réussit à la rendre tolérante. Bonnivard engagea le Conseil à accorder un tems suffisant pour examiner les propositions qu'on leur faisait; il réussit par sa douceur: on prêche toujours le Christianisme avec succès quand on le prêche avec charité....

"Bonnivard fut savant: ses manuscrits, qui sont dans la bibliothèque publique, prouvent qu'il avait bien lu les auteurs classiques Latins, et qu'il avait approfondi la théologie et l'histoire. Ce grand homme aimait les sciences, et il croyait qu'elles pouvaient faire la gloire de Genève; aussi il ne négligea rien pour les fixer dans cette ville naissante; en 1551 il donna sa bibliothèque au public; elle fut le commencement de notre bibliothèque publique; et ces livres sont en partie les rares et belles éditions du quinzième siècle qu'on voit dans notre collection. Enfin, pendant la même année, ce bon patriote institua la République son héritière, à condition qu'elle employerait ses biens à entretenir le collège dont on projettait la fondation.

"Il parait que Bonnivard mourut en 1570; mais on ne peut l'assurer, parcequ'il y a une lacune dans le Nécrologe depuis le mois de Juillet, 1570, jusques en 1571." —

THE PRISONER OF CHILLON

I.
MY hair is grey, but not with years,
Nor grew it white
In a single night,
As men's have grown from sudden fears:
My limbs are bowed, though not with toil,
But rusted with a vile repose,
For they have been a dungeon's spoil,
And mine has been the fate of those
To whom the goodly earth and air
Are banned, and barred — forbidden fare;10
But this was for my father's faith
I suffered chains and courted death;
That father perished at the stake
For tenets he would not forsake;
And for the same his lineal race
In darkness found a dwelling place;
We were seven — who now are one,
Six in youth, and one in age,
Finished as they had begun,
Proud of Persecution's rage;20
One in fire, and two in field,
Their belief with blood have sealed,
Dying as their father died,
For the God their foes denied; —
Three were in a dungeon cast,
Of whom this wreck is left the last.
II.
There are seven pillars of Gothic mould,
In Chillon's dungeons deep and old,

There are seven columns, massy and grey,
Dim with a dull imprisoned ray,30
A sunbeam which hath lost its way,
And through the crevice and the cleft
Of the thick wall is fallen and left;
Creeping o'er the floor so damp,
Like a marsh's meteor lamp:
And in each pillar there is a ring,
And in each ring there is a chain;
That iron is a cankering thing,
For in these limbs its teeth remain,
With marks that will not wear away,40
Till I have done with this new day,
Which now is painful to these eyes,
Which have not seen the sun so rise
For years—I cannot count them o'er,
I lost their long and heavy score
When my last brother drooped and died,
And I lay living by his side.
III.
They chained us each to a column stone,
And we were three—yet, each alone;
We could not move a single pace,50
We could not see each other's face,
But with that pale and livid light
That made us strangers in our sight:
And thus together—yet apart,
Fettered in hand, but joined in heart,
'Twas still some solace in the dearth
Of the pure elements of earth,
To hearken to each other's speech,
And each turn comforter to each
With some new hope, or legend old,60
Or song heroically bold;
But even these at length grew cold.

Our voices took a dreary tone,
An echo of the dungeon stone,
A grating sound, not full and free,
As they of yore were wont to be:
It might be fancy — but to me
They never sounded like our own.
IV.
I was the eldest of the three,
And to uphold and cheer the rest70
I ought to do — and did my best —
And each did well in his degree.
The youngest, whom my father loved,
Because our mother's brow was given
To him, with eyes as blue as heaven —
For him my soul was sorely moved:
And truly might it be distressed
To see such bird in such a nest;
For he was beautiful as day —
(When day was beautiful to me80
As to young eagles, being free) —
A polar day, which will not see
A sunset till its summer's gone,
Its sleepless summer of long light,
The snow-clad offspring of the sun:
And thus he was as pure and bright,
And in his natural spirit gay,
With tears for nought but others' ills,
And then they flowed like mountain rills,
Unless he could assuage the woe90
Which he abhorred to view below.
V.
The other was as pure of mind,
But formed to combat with his kind;
Strong in his frame, and of a mood
Which 'gainst the world in war had stood,

And perished in the foremost rank
With joy:—but not in chains to pine:
His spirit withered with their clank,
I saw it silently decline—
And so perchance in sooth did mine:100
But yet I forced it on to cheer
Those relics of a home so dear.
He was a hunter of the hills,
Had followed there the deer and wolf;
To him this dungeon was a gulf,
And fettered feet the worst of ills.
VI.
Lake Leman lies by Chillon's walls:
A thousand feet in depth below
Its massy waters meet and flow;
Thus much the fathom-line was sent110
From Chillon's snow-white battlement,
Which round about the wave inthralls:
A double dungeon wall and wave
Have made—and like a living grave.
Below the surface of the lake
The dark vault lies wherein we lay:
We heard it ripple night and day;
Sounding o'er our heads it knocked;
And I have felt the winter's spray
Wash through the bars when winds were high120
And wanton in the happy sky;
And then the very rock hath rocked,
And I have felt it shake, unshocked,
Because I could have smiled to see
The death that would have set me free.
VII.
I said my nearer brother pined,
I said his mighty heart declined,
He loathed and put away his food;

It was not that 'twas coarse and rude,
For we were used to hunter's fare,130
And for the like had little care:
The milk drawn from the mountain goat
Was changed for water from the moat,
Our bread was such as captives' tears
Have moistened many a thousand years,
Since man first pent his fellow men
Like brutes within an iron den;
But what were these to us or him?
These wasted not his heart or limb;
My brother's soul was of that mould140
Which in a palace had grown cold,
Had his free breathing been denied
The range of the steep mountain's side;
But why delay the truth? — he died.
I saw, and could not hold his head,
Nor reach his dying hand — nor dead, —
Though hard I strove, but strove in vain,
To rend and gnash my bonds in twain.
He died — and they unlocked his chain,
And scooped for him a shallow grave150
Even from the cold earth of our cave.
I begged them, as a boon, to lay
His corse in dust whereon the day
Might shine — it was a foolish thought,
But then within my brain it wrought,
That even in death his freeborn breast
In such a dungeon could not rest.
I might have spared my idle prayer —
They coldly laughed — and laid him there:
The flat and turfless earth above160
The being we so much did love;
His empty chain above it leant,
Such Murder's fitting monument!

VIII.
But he, the favourite and the flower,
Most cherished since his natal hour,
His mother's image in fair face,
The infant love of all his race,
His martyred father's dearest thought,
My latest care, for whom I sought
To hoard my life, that his might be170
Less wretched now, and one day free;
He, too, who yet had held untired
A spirit natural or inspired —
He, too, was struck, and day by day
Was withered on the stalk away.
Oh, God! it is a fearful thing
To see the human soul take wing
In any shape, in any mood:
I've seen it rushing forth in blood,
I've seen it on the breaking ocean180
Strive with a swoln convulsive motion,
I've seen the sick and ghastly bed
Of Sin delirious with its dread:
But these were horrors — this was woe
Unmixed with such — but sure and slow:
He faded, and so calm and meek,
So softly worn, so sweetly weak,
So tearless, yet so tender — kind,
And grieved for those he left behind;
With all the while a cheek whose bloom190
Was as a mockery of the tomb,
Whose tints as gently sunk away
As a departing rainbow's ray;
An eye of most transparent light,
That almost made the dungeon bright;
And not a word of murmur — not
A groan o'er his untimely lot, —

A little talk of better days,
A little hope my own to raise,
For I was sunk in silence — lost200
In this last loss, of all the most;
And then the sighs he would suppress
Of fainting Nature's feebleness,
More slowly drawn, grew less and less:
I listened, but I could not hear;
I called, for I was wild with fear;
I knew 'twas hopeless, but my dread
Would not be thus admonished;
I called, and thought I heard a sound —
I burst my chain with one strong bound,210
And rushed to him: — I found him not,
I only stirred in this black spot,
I only lived, I only drew
The accursed breath of dungeon-dew;
The last, the sole, the dearest link
Between me and the eternal brink,
Which bound me to my failing race,
Was broken in this fatal place.
One on the earth, and one beneath —
My brothers — both had ceased to breathe:220
I took that hand which lay so still,
Alas! my own was full as chill;
I had not strength to stir, or strive,
But felt that I was still alive —
A frantic feeling, when we know
That what we love shall ne'er be so.
I know not why
I could not die,
I had no earthly hope — but faith,
And that forbade a selfish death.230

IX.

What next befell me then and there
I know not well — I never knew —
First came the loss of light, and air,
And then of darkness too:
I had no thought, no feeling — none —
Among the stones I stood a stone,
And was, scarce conscious what I wist,
As shrubless crags within the mist;
For all was blank, and bleak, and grey;
It was not night — it was not day;240
It was not even the dungeon-light,
So hateful to my heavy sight,
But vacancy absorbing space,
And fixedness — without a place;
There were no stars — no earth — no time —
No check — no change — no good — no crime —
But silence, and a stirless breath
Which neither was of life nor death;
A sea of stagnant idleness,
Blind, boundless, mute, and motionless!250
X.
A light broke in upon my brain, —
It was the carol of a bird;
It ceased, and then it came again,
The sweetest song ear ever heard,
And mine was thankful till my eyes
Ran over with the glad surprise,
And they that moment could not see
I was the mate of misery;
But then by dull degrees came back
My senses to their wonted track;260
I saw the dungeon walls and floor
Close slowly round me as before,
I saw the glimmer of the sun
Creeping as it before had done,

But through the crevice where it came
That bird was perched, as fond and tame,
And tamer than upon the tree;
A lovely bird, with azure wings,
And song that said a thousand things,
And seemed to say them all for me!270
I never saw its like before,
I ne'er shall see its likeness more:
It seemed like me to want a mate,
But was not half so desolate,
And it was come to love me when
None lived to love me so again,
And cheering from my dungeon's brink,
Had brought me back to feel and think.
I know not if it late were free,
Or broke its cage to perch on mine,280
But knowing well captivity,
Sweet bird! I could not wish for thine!
Or if it were, in wingéd guise,
A visitant from Paradise;
For — Heaven forgive that thought! the while
Which made me both to weep and smile —
I sometimes deemed that it might be
My brother's soul come down to me;
But then at last away it flew,
And then 'twas mortal well I knew,290
For he would never thus have flown —
And left me twice so doubly lone, —
Lone — as the corse within its shroud,
Lone — as a solitary cloud,
A single cloud on a sunny day,
While all the rest of heaven is clear,
A frown upon the atmosphere,
That hath no business to appear
When skies are blue, and earth is gay.

XI.
A kind of change came in my fate,300
My keepers grew compassionate;
I know not what had made them so,
They were inured to sights of woe,
But so it was: — my broken chain
With links unfastened did remain,
And it was liberty to stride
Along my cell from side to side,
And up and down, and then athwart,
And tread it over every part;
And round the pillars one by one,310
Returning where my walk begun,
Avoiding only, as I trod,
My brothers' graves without a sod;
For if I thought with heedless tread
My step profaned their lowly bed,
My breath came gaspingly and thick,
And my crushed heart felt blind and sick.
XII.
I made a footing in the wall,
It was not therefrom to escape,
For I had buried one and all,320
Who loved me in a human shape;
And the whole earth would henceforth be
A wider prison unto me:
No child — no sire — no kin had I,
No partner in my misery;
I thought of this, and I was glad,
For thought of them had made me mad;
But I was curious to ascend
To my barred windows, and to bend
Once more, upon the mountains high,330
The quiet of a loving eye.
XIII.

I saw them—and they were the same,
They were not changed like me in frame;
I saw their thousand years of snow
On high—their wide long lake below,
And the blue Rhone in fullest flow;
I heard the torrents leap and gush
O'er channelled rock and broken bush;
I saw the white-walled distant town,
And whiter sails go skimming down;340
And then there was a little isle,
Which in my very face did smile,
The only one in view;
A small green isle, it seemed no more,
Scarce broader than my dungeon floor,
But in it there were three tall trees,
And o'er it blew the mountain breeze,
And by it there were waters flowing,
And on it there were young flowers growing,
Of gentle breath and hue.350
The fish swam by the castle wall,
And they seemed joyous each and all;
The eagle rode the rising blast,
Methought he never flew so fast
As then to me he seemed to fly;
And then new tears came in my eye,
And I felt troubled—and would fain
I had not left my recent chain;
And when I did descend again,
The darkness of my dim abode360
Fell on me as a heavy load;
It was as is a new-dug grave,
Closing o'er one we sought to save,—
And yet my glance, too much opprest,
Had almost need of such a rest.

XIV.
It might be months, or years, or days—
I kept no count, I took no note—
I had no hope my eyes to raise,
And clear them of their dreary mote;
At last men came to set me free;370
I asked not why, and recked not where;
It was at length the same to me,
Fettered or fetterless to be,
I learned to love despair.
And thus when they appeared at last,
And all my bonds aside were cast,
These heavy walls to me had grown
A hermitage—and all my own!
And half I felt as they were come
To tear me from a second home:380
With spiders I had friendship made,
And watched them in their sullen trade,
Had seen the mice by moonlight play,
And why should I feel less than they?
We were all inmates of one place,
And I, the monarch of each race,
Had power to kill—yet, strange to tell!
In quiet we had learned to dwell;
My very chains and I grew friends,
So much a long communion tends390
To make us what we are:—even I
Regained my freedom with a sigh.

41530903R00016

Made in the USA
San Bernardino, CA
03 July 2019